THE LITTLE RED WHITE AND BLUE BOOK

THE LITTLE RED WHITE & WHITE & BLUE BOOK

Johnny (Appleseed) Rossen

GROVE PRESS, INC.
NEW YORK

CONTENTS

Foreword ....

I. Right of Revolution 1

II. Property and the Class Struggle 12

III. The Working Class 27

IV. Black Liberation 35

V. War, Militarism and
   Imperialism 51

VI. Women's Liberation 61

VII. Students and Schools 68

VIII. The Press 73

IX. On Voting 75

X. Patriotism 77

XI. Liberals and Liberalism 80

XII. Law and Order 85

XIII. Self Defense and Violence 91

XIV. Dare to Struggle 98

FOREWORD

There is nothing more common than to confound the terms of the American Revolution with those of the late American war. The American war is over but this is far from being the case with the American Revolution. On the contrary, nothing but the first act of the great drama is closed.

Benjamin Rush, 1787

We are the true Americans reborn at a time when it is almost a crime to be truly American. Those creeps who drove by the church in a Cadillac waving an American flag and calling coward, why, they don't even know what it is to be an American. I say it is a crime for them to misuse such spirit. Only the raggle-taggles of it is theirs, because while we burned those cards with our hands—we carried that spirit in our hearts.

Wayne Hansen,
Draft-card burner, 1967

One hundred and eighty years separate these statements of Benjamin Rush and Wayne Hansen—of the Revolutionary war and the street battles of Stop-The-Draft Week in Oakland, Cal.

But the two are part of the continuing struggle that Rush spoke of—the continuing American Revolution.

It did not take long for the privileged ruling class to suffocate the spirit of the true American Revolution—to force it underground . . . to rob its trappings and symbols, its slogans and flags, and transform them into the symbols of supernationalist greed and exploitation.

But the exploiters—then and now—could never really slay the spirit of change.

The dominant theme of America may be one of ugly exploitation by the few of the many. But American history also has a strong and vigorous radical undercurrent—one that has opposed and resisted the forces who turned the noble experiment into a slaughterhouse of greed and racism which keeps colonies at home and maintains an empire abroad.

This short book of quotations from Americans, past and present, is aimed at accelerating the battle to reclaim America and restore its revolutionary spirit as the nation's dominant force.

The Little Red White and Blue Book is, of course, inspired—but not modeled after—Chairman Mao's "Little Red Book" of quotations for revolutionaries. It is in no way intended to mock or satirize Mao's powerful collection.

Its sole intention is to acquaint American radicals with their American roots—to inspire and, perhaps, instruct those actively seeking to continue the Revolution that was betrayed 180 years ago.

America's radicals are conditioned to despise their country—to look elsewhere for their inspiration and guidance. That is because the history of the radicals' "other America" or "Under-America" is neglected or grossly distorted by our schools. The radicals who do penetrate into the schools' homogenized textbooks are distorted beyond recognition. School children are rarely given a sense of their struggle.

How many of us were taught that Helen Keller not only engaged in heroic battle against her blindness but also against American capitalism? Not only was she a socialist, but a member of the revolutionary Industrial Workers of the World, the "wobblies."

Did Dwight Eisenhower know that Honus Wagner, baseball great and his boyhood hero, was also a socialist?

Do any of us realize that May Day—which our rulers try to picture as a European Communist holiday—was first celebrated as a day of worker protest in Chicago during the violent labor struggles of the 1880s?

Who has been taught that the concept of inevitable class struggle—laborers versus bosses; oppressed against oppressors—emerged in America long before Karl Marx was born?

And what about the symbol of Uncle Sam? Now it stands as a symbol of strident imperialism or of the tyrant who runs the draft and "wants you." But he was originally a symbol of the first American revolutionaries.

Like the flag, Uncle Sam was taken from us—wrenched away by the robbing class to camouflage more robbing.

The rulers who run our schools have convinced us that America's traditions belong to them—that radicalism and the right to revolution are foreign concepts, strangers to our shores.

This book, if it does little else, should destroy that historical mutation. This book should illuminate the wisdom of Marxist historian Charles Beard, who once said:

"One of the best ways to get yourself a reputation as a dangerous citizen . . . is to go about repeating the very phrases which our founding fathers used in the great struggle for independence."

This book will inspire more than it will instruct. It is not a treatise of tactics or even of strategy. It is a primer of protest. By no means should it be considered a complete collection of America's radical quotations. Most readers most probably will have a favorite quotation that is not included in this slim volume.

The Little Red White and Blue Book is aimed at redressing the balance of what is considered quotable, which up to now has swum in the syrup of sublime thoughts and "wise" words. The words of Americans have been filled with fire and anger, with dry wit and melancholy and unconscious condemnation. Few of these words are remembered by the official "rememberers" who concoct our schoolbooks, where all men wear wigs, powder their noses and speak in platitudes. It is time to see the other side of the American coin.

I. RIGHT OF REVOLUTION

When in the course of human events it becomes necessary for one people to dissolve the political bonds which have connected them with another, and to assume among the powers of the earth the separate and equal station to which the laws of nature and of nature's God entitle them, a decent respect to the opinions of mankind requires that they should declare the causes which impel them to separation.

We hold these truths to be self-evident; that all men are created equal; that they are endowed by their Creator with inherent and inalienable rights; that among these are life, liberty, and the pursuit of happiness; that to secure these rights, governments are instituted among men, deriving their just powers from the consent of the governed; that whenever any form of government becomes destructive of these ends, it is the right of the people to alter or abolish it, and to institute new government, laying its foundation on such principles, and organizing its powers in such form as to them shall seem most likely to effect their safety and happiness.

Declaration of Independence, 1776,
Black Panther Party, 1967

God forbid we should ever be twenty years without . . . a rebellion.

Thomas Jefferson, 1787

The tree of liberty must be refreshed from time to time with the blood of patriots and tyrants. It is their natural manure.

Thomas Jefferson, 1787

It is an observation of one of the profoundest inquiries into human affairs that a revolution of government is the strongest proof that can be given by a people, of their virtue and good sense.

John Adams

As revolutions have begun, it is natural to expect that other revolutions will follow.

Thomas Paine, 1791

In the abstract theory of our government the obedience of the citizen is not due to an unconstitutional law: he may lawfully resist its execution.

John Quincy Adams

An oppressed people are authorized whenever they can to rise and break their fetters.

Henry Clay, politician, 1818

If the State cannot survive the . . . agitation, then let the State perish. If the Church must be cast down by the strugglings of Humanity to be free, then let the American Union be consumed by a living thunderbolt, and no tear shed over its ashes. If the Republic must be blotted out from the roll of nations, by proclaiming liberty to the captives, then let the Republic sink beneath the waves of oblivion, and a shout of joy, louder than the voice of many waters, fill the universe at its extinction.

William Lloyd Garrison, 1840

Any people anywhere, being inclined and having the power, have the right to rise up and shake off the existing government and form a new one that suits them better. This is a most valuable and sacred right—a right we hope and believe is to liberate the world.

Abraham Lincoln, 1848

Revolution is the only thing, the only power, that ever worked out freedom for any people. The powers that have ruled long, and learned to love ruling, will never give up that prerogative till they find they must, till they see the certainty of overthrow and destruction if they do not! . . . To plant—to revolutionize—those are the twin stars that have ruled our pathway. What have we then to dread in the word Revolution—we, the children of rebels! We were born to be rebels—it runs in the blood.

Wendell Phillips, 1848

All men recognize the right of revolution; that is, the right to refuse allegiance to, and to resist, the government, when its tyranny and its inefficiency are great and unendurable . . . All machines have their friction. But when the friction comes to have its machine, and oppression and robbery are organized, I say, let us not have such a machine any longer.

Henry David Thoreau, 1849

If by the mere force of numbers a majority should deprive a minority of any clearly written constitutional rights, it might, in a moral point of view, justify revolution—certainly would if such a right were a vital one.

Abraham Lincoln, 1861

This country, with its institutions, belongs to the people who inhabit it. When-

ever they shall grow weary of the existing government, they can exercise their
constitutional right of amending it, or
their revolutionary right to dismember or
overthrow it.

Abraham Lincoln, 1861

If we do not soon bestir ourselves for a
bloody revolution, we cannot leave anything to our children but poverty and
slavery.

Die Arbeiter Zeitung,
Chicago labor paper, 1886

Full opportunity for full development
is the unalienable right of all. He who
denies it is a tyrant, he who does not demand it is a coward; he who is indifferent to it is a slave; he who does not desire it is dead. The earth for all the people! That is the demand.

Eugene Debs, 1904

The most heroic word in all languages is—REVOLUTION!

Eugene Debs, 1907

We can't have education without revolution. We have tried peace education for 1,900 years and it has failed. Let us try revolution and see what it will do now.

Helen Keller, 1916

Those who won our independence by revolution were not cowards. They did not fear political change. They did not exalt order at the cost of liberty.

Louis Brandeis,
Supreme Court Justice, 1927

Wherever one goes in this civilized world, one always finds the same set-up. The little man, the man who does the dirty work, the producer is of no importance, receives no consideration and is always being asked to make the greatest sacrifice. Yet everything depends on this forgotten man. Not a wheel could turn without his support and co-operation. It is this man, whose number is legion, who has no voice in world affairs . . . he knows that he has been robbed and cheated from time immemorial. He is suffocated with all this bitter knowledge. He waits and waits hoping that time will alter things. And slowly he realizes that time alters nothing, that with time things only grow worse. One day, he will decide to act. "Wait!" he will be told. "Wait just a little longer." But he will refuse to wait another second.

Henry Miller, 1947

That circumstances sometimes justify it . . . (revolution) is not Communist doctrine but an old American belief.

Justice Jackson, 1950

There is a political feudalism where a dynasty has the trappings of a parliamentary system but manipulates it for the benefit of the ruling class . . . Revolution in the twentieth century means rebellion against another kind of feudalism . . . economic feudalism . . . and the United States should promote democratic revolution against these conditions of economic feudalism.

William Douglas,
Supreme Court Justice

They set up the courts; they set up the police; they set up the army; they set up an educational system; they set up the newspaper; they set up all the apparatus to brainwash and to keep in subjugation. If we're going to be free, and we will not be fully free until we smash this state completely and totally . . . no people in this world have ever achieved independence and freedom through the ballot or having it legislated to them. (They) got their freedom through struggle and through revolution.

William Epton, 1964

I consider myself neither legally nor morally bound to obey laws made by a body in which I have no representation. Do not deceive yourselves into believing that penalties will deter men from the course they believe is right. We stand on the eve of a BLACK REVOLUTION.

H. Rap. Brown, 1967

II. PROPERTY AND THE CLASS STRUGGLE

The poverty of the country is such that all the power and sway has got into the hands of the rich, who by extortious advantages, having the common people in their debt, have always curbed and oppressed them in all manner of ways.

Nathaniel Bacon,
Rebel leader, 1676

No man is naturally entitled to a greater porportion of the earth than another . . . (Land) was made for the equal use of all.

Pennsylvania farmers, 1740s

In every society where property exists there will ever be a struggle between rich and poor. Mixed in one assembly, equal laws can never be expected.

John Adams

Private Property . . . is a Creature of Society, and is subject to the Calls of that Society, whenever its Necessities shall require it, even to its last Farthing.

Benjamin Franklin, 1783

. . . the earth in its uncultivated state was, and ever would have continued to be, the common property of the human race.

Thomas Paine, 1776

The most common and durable source of faction has been the various and unequal distribution of property.

James Madison,
The Federalist, No. 10

There has been an actual struggle between the labouring part of the Community and those lazy rascals that have invented every means the Devil has put into their heads to destroy the labouring parts of the Community.

Anon pamphleteer, 1800

There appear to exist two distinct classes, the rich and the poor; the oppressed and the oppressor; those that live by their own labor and they that live by the labor of others; the aristocratic and the democratic; the despotic and republican, who are in direct opposition to one another in their objects and pursuits.

Working Men's Republican
Political Assn. Penn Township,
Pa., 1830s

Even if we grant that the American has freed himself from a political tyrant, he is still the slave of an economical and moral tyrant.

Henry David Thoreau

These capitalists generally act harmoniously, and in concert, to fleece the people.

Abraham Lincoln, 1837

Following the destruction of the banks, must come that of all monopolies, of all PRIVILEGE. There are many of these. We cannot specify them all; we therefore select only one, the greatest of them all, the privilege which some have of being born rich while others are born poor. It will be seen at once that we allude to the hereditary descent of property, an anomaly in our American system, which must be removed, or the system itself will be destroyed.

Orestes Brownson, 1840

15

The great and fruitful source of crime and misery on earth is the inequality of society—the abject dependence of honest willing industry upon idle and dishonest capitalists.

U.S. Rep. Mike Walsh,
Irish-American, 1840

Things are in the saddle
And ride mankind

Ralph Waldo Emerson, 1847

Absolutely speaking, the more money the less virtue; for money comes between a man and his objects and obtains them for him; and it was certainly no great virtue to obtain it.

Henry David Thoreau, 1849

Whenever there is a conflict between human rights and property rights, human rights must prevail.

Abraham Lincoln

It seems that . . . property has become much more sacred and the guarantees of the Constitution protect it much more efficiently than they do the life or liberty of the citizen.

Illinois Senator Trumbull,
19th Century

We cannot go on prating of the inalienable rights of man and then denying the inalienable right to the bounty of the Creator.

Henry George, 1879

Who are the oppressors? The few: the king, the capitalist and a handful of other overseers and superintendents. Who are the oppressed? The many: the nations of the earth; the valuable personages; the workers; they that make the bread that the soft-handed and idle eat. Why is it right that there is not a fairer division of the spoil all around? Because laws and constitutions have ordered otherwise. Then it follows that laws and constitutions should change around and say there shall be a more nearly equal division.

Mark Twain, 1886

There are ninety and nine who live and
   die
In want and hunger and cold
That one may live in luxury
And be wrapped in a silken fold
The ninety and nine in hovels bare
The one in a palace with riches rare

And the one owns cities and houses and
   lands
And the ninety and nine have empty
   hands

Farmer's Alliance, 1889

Wall Street owns the country. It is no longer a government of the people, by the people and for the people, but a government of Wall Street, by Wall Street and for Wall Street.

Mary Lease,
Kansas populist, 1890

The great common people of this country are slaves, and monopoly is their master. Our laws are the output of a system which clothes rascals in robes and honesty in rags . . . We will stand by our homes and stay by our firesides by force if necessary. The people are at bay, let the bloodhounds of money who have dogged us thus far beware.

Elizabeth Barr,
Kansas agitator, 1890

The plutocracy today is the logical result of the individual freedom which we have always considered to be the pride of our system. . . . The corporation has absorbed the community. The community must now absorb the corporation. A stage must be reached in which each is for all and all is for each.

Lincoln (Neb.) Farmers
Alliance, 1890s

This government was founded by plain men, not millionaires. But we now have two parties arrayed against each other, Aristocracy against Commonality. Thirty thousand families own one half the wealth of the country, and they have no part in producing it. They have stolen it from the labor and toil that has produced the nation.

Ignatius Donnelly, 1894
Populist orator

There is no man who has an ounce of honesty in his make-up but recognizes the fact that there is a continuous struggle between the two classes.

Big Bill Haywood, June 27, 1905

I would not be a capitalist; I would be a man; you cannot be both at the same time.

Eugene Debs, 1905

The country is governed for the richest, for the corporations, the bankers, the land speculators, and for the exploiters of labor.

Helen Keller, 1911

The truth is we are all caught in a great economic system which is heartless.

Woodrow Wilson, 1912

You can't wear the Social Register for waterwings.

> Mrs. Margaret (The Unsinkable Molly) Brown, 1912, after the sinking of the Titanic

Now the boss works for the capitalist. Under Socialism, he will work for YOU. You will elect him and if he isn't satisfactory you will fire him and get another.

> A. W. Rickes, Labor organizer, 1914

I am opposing a social order in which it is possible for one man who does absolutely nothing that is useful to amass a fortune of millions of dollars—while millions of men and women who work all the days of their lives secure barely enough for a wretched existence.

> Eugene Debs, 1918

In very truth gold is god today and rules with pitiless sway in the affairs of men.

Eugene Debs, 1918

Private appropriation of the earth's surface, the natural resources and the means of life is nothing less than a crime against humanity, but the . . . few who are the beneficiaries of this iniquitous social arrangement, far from being viewed as criminals meriting punishment, are the exalted rulers of society, and the people they exploit gladly render them homage and obeisance.

Eugene Debs, 1927

The economic owning class is always the political ruling class.

Eugene Debs, 1927

Don't get the idea that I'm one of these
goddam radicals. Don't get the idea that
I'm knocking the American system.

Al Capone, gangster, 1929

The people shrink titans into dwarfs
The honorable orators, the gazettes of
    thunder,
The tycoons, big shots, and dictators
Flicker in the mirrors a few moments
And fade through the glass of death
For discussion in an autocracy of worms.

While the rootholds of the earth nourish
    the majestic people
Shouting unimagined shibboleths and
    slogans
Tracing their heels in moth-eaten insig-
    nia of bawdy leaders
Piling revolt on revolt across night valleys
Letting loose insurrections, uprisings,
    strikes

24

Marches, mass-meetings, banners, de-
    clared resolves.
Plodding in a somnambulism of fog and
    rain
Til a given moment exploded by long-
    prepared events.

Carl Sandburg, "The People, Yes"

Private enterprise is ceasing to be free
enterprise.

Franklin D. Roosevelt, 1938

The elite cannot be truly thought of as
men who are merely "doing their duty"
. . . they are the ones who determine their
duty, as well as the duties of other men.

C. Wright Mills, 1958

If there was one thing that started me
thinking it was President (Franklin)
Roosevelt's cufflinks . . . Some of them

with rubies and precious stones . . . and I'll never forget I was sitting on an old tire out in the front yard and we were poor and hungry. I was sitting out there in the hot sun. There weren't any trees and I was wondering why it is that one man could have all those cufflinks when we couldn't have enough to eat.

Peggy Terry,
Welfare rights organizer

Money doesn't talk, it swears.

Bob Dylan, folksinger

Power goes to two poles—to those who've got the money and those who've got people.

Saul Alinsky, agitator, 1966

III. THE WORKING CLASS

The working classes have taken the field and never will give up the contest until the power that oppresses them is annihilated.

Working Man's Advocate, 1809

How can we be free while we have no control over the only commodity we have to dispose of—our labor?

Journeymen Cordwainers of
New York, 1836

Brothers, shall we content ourselves with the miserable idea of merely saving a few dollars and say we have found enough? Future generations, aye, the uprising generation is looking to us for nobler deeds . . . We must proceed . . . to joint ownership in God's earth, the foundation that our edifice must stand upon.

New England Protective Union,
1830s

We do not believe there can be a single person found east of the mountains who ever thanked God for permission to work in a cotton mill.

Seth Luther, labor agitator, 1830s

Let us be determined no longer to be deceived by the cry of those who produce nothing and who enjoy all, and who insultingly term us—the farmers, mechanics and the laborers—the lower orders and exultingly claim our homage for themselves as the higher orders—while ourselves as the higher orders—while the Declaration of Independence asserts that "all men are created equal."

Seth Luther, 1830s

By the old system we have no time for mental cultivation—that is the policy of the big bugs—they endeavor to keep people ignorant by keeping them always at work.

Boston worker, 1835

Labor is prior to and independent of capital. Capital is only the fruit of labor, and could never have existed if labor had not first existed. Labor is the superior of capital, and man deserves much the higher consideration.

Abraham Lincoln, 1861

One thing is certain; that of the amount actually produced by the operative, he retains a less proportion than it costs the master to feed, clothe and lodge his slave. Wages is a cunning device to the devil, for the benefit of tender consciences who would retain all the advantages of the slave system, without his expense, trouble and odium of being slave holders.

Orestes Brownson, Boston, 1850

If labor mainly . . . serves the purpose of a police, to keep men out of mischief, it indicates a rottenness at the foundation of our community.

Henry David Thoreau, 1859

I can hire one half of the working class to kill the other half.

Jay Gould, robber baron,
19th Century

The man who is the enemy of the black laboring man is the enemy of the white laboring man the world over. The same influences that go to keep down and crush down the rights of the poor black man bear down and oppress the poor white laboring man.

Henry Wilson, U.S. Senator, 1863

After God had finished the rattlesnake, the toad and the vampire, he had some awful substance left with which He made a SCAB. A SCAB is a two-legged animal with a corkscrew soul, a water-logged brain and a combination backbone made of jelly and glue. Where others have hearts he carries a tumor of rotten principles. A strikebreaker is a traitor to his God, his country, his family and his class!

Jack London, author, 1904

To talk about reforming rotten graft-infested (A.F.of L.) Unions, which are dominated absolutely by the labor boss, is as vain and wasteful as to spray a cesspool with attar of roses.

Big Bill Haywood, I.W.W. 1905

The old form of trade unionism no longer meets the demands of the working class . . . It is now positively reactionary, and is maintained not in the interests of the workers who support it but in the interests of the capitalist class who exploit the workers.

Eugene Debs, 1905

Either the whites organize with the Negroes, or the bosses will organize the Negroes against the whites, in which last case it is hardly up to the whites to 'damn the niggers.'

I.W.W.'s "Appeal to Lumber Workers," 1912

We recognize that the question of race superiority injected into the minds of the white wage worker against the Negro . . . is only a tactical method used in the capitalist class to keep the workers divided.

Tennessee Socialists, 1912

When the Union's inspiration through the worker's blood shall run,
There can be no power greater anywhere beneath the sun,
Yet what force on earth is weaker than the feeble strength of one?
But the union makes us strong.

Ralph Chaplin, Jan. 17, 1915
Song, *Solidarity Forever*

We hate their rotten system more than any mortals do
Our aim is not to patch it up, but build it all anew.

And what we'll have for government,
when finally we're through
 Is one Big Industrial Union!

> Ralph Chaplin, little-known verse
> to *Solidarity Forever*

The cause of the workingmen is the cause of the country.

> *Working Man's Advocate*
> April 30, 1930

IV. BLACK
LIBERATION

I have nothing more to offer than what George Washington would have had to offer had he been taken by the British officers and put to trial by them. I have ventured my life in endeavoring to obtain the freedom of my countrymen. I know that you have pre-determined to shed my blood. Why then all this mockery of a trial?

A slave during Gabriel's Revolt, 1800

They think because they hold us in infernal chains of slavery that we wish to be white, or of their color, but they are

dreadfully deceived—we wish to be just
as it pleased our creator to have made us.

David Walker,
Black abolitionist, 1828

Brethren, the time has come when you
must act for yourselves! If you must
bleed, let it all come at once—rather die
freemen than live to be slaves!

Henry Highland Garnet,
Black leader, 1843

I got massa's confidence and worked
well and obeyed him well, and I talked to
the niggers before him, in a way to please
him. But they could understand me, for I
had been doing missionary work among
them, and the neighbors' niggers too, but
not such missionary work as massa'
thought I was doing.

Anonymous fugitive slave,
returned to the plantation
to get his family away.

For a white man to defend his friend unto blood is praiseworthy but for a black man to do precisely the same thing is a crime. It was glorious for Americans to drench the soil and crimson the sea with blood to escape payment of threepenny tax upon tea; but it is a crime to shoot down a monster in defense of the liberty of a black man and to save him from bondage one minute of which (in the language of Jefferson) is worse than ages of that which our fathers rose in rebellion to oppose.

Frederick Douglass, 1854

Let us develop our manhood, not by folding our arms together and keeping out of sight, while all the oppressed Nations of the earth are struggling to be free, but let us ever remember that "They who would be free, Themselves must strike the first blow."

Frederick Douglass, 1855

37

To float quietly with the current, allowing others to win and bestow the freedom which we lazily propose to enjoy, will go far to prove the charges of our enemies are true, and sink us lower in the estimation of our white countrymen. The Open Sesame for the colored man is action! Action! Action!

Frederick Douglass, 1856

I wish to say, furthermore, that you had better, all you people of the South, prepare yourselves for a settlement of that question, that must come up for settlement sooner than you are prepared for it. The sooner you are prepared the better. You may dispose of me very easily. I am nearly disposed of now; but this question, is still to be settled—This Negro question, I mean; the end of that is not yet!

John Brown, 1859

It was his peculiar doctrine that a man has a perfect right to interfere by force with the slaveholder, in order to rescue the slave. I agree with him.

Henry David Thoreau, Lecture,
"A Plea For John Brown," 1859

Slaves are generally expected to sing as well as to work.

Frederick Douglass

Sleepy people don't like to be disturbed. They hate the trouble-maker, call him names, draw their curtains, close their blinds, turn their backs to the light—but the sun rises nevertheless, and the most conservative HUNKER of them all is compelled to acknowledge it.

Frederick Douglass, 1863

The employers retain the power to starve them (Negroes) to death and wherever this power is held, there is the power of slavery.

Frederick Douglass, 1865

Assault compels defense. I shall never ask the colored people to be lambs where the whites insist upon being wolves, and yet no man shall outdo me in efforts to promote kindness . . . between the races. But I know there can be no peace without justice, and hence the sword.

Frederick Douglass, 1871

The white man writes his history for us to study, makes his scenario with his heroes and heroines for us to admire and supplies our newspapers. Through these instrumentalities, he almost controls our thought . . . If we believe that we come from nowhere and have no history but that of a slave, our substance will be the charity of our oppressors and our future handicapped by doubts and fears.

Prospectus of Ancient Order of
Ethiopian Princes, Chicago, 1921

Two hundred and fifty years we have been a race of slaves; for fifty years we have been a race of parasites. Now we propose to end all that. No more fear, no more cringing, no more sycophantic begging and pleading; the Negro must strike straight from the shoulder for manhood rights and full liberty.

Marcus Garvey, 1921

. . . those brave ones who struggle against death are the ones who bring new life into the world, even though they die to do so, even though our hearts are broken when they die.

Richard Wright, writer

You are either a victim or a rebel.

Richard Wright

There shall come a day when we pour out our hearts over this land.

Richard Wright

A man who won't die for something is not fit to live.

Martin Luther King, 1961

The existence of violence is at the very heart of a racist system . . . When people say they are opposed to Negroes "resorting to violence" what they really mean is that they are opposed to Negroes defending themselves and challenging the exclusive monopoly of violent practices by white racists.

Robert Williams,
Black nationalist, 1962

When we let freedom ring, when we let it ring from every village and every hamlet, from every state and every city, we will be able to speed up that day when all of God's Children, black men and white men, Jews and Gentiles, Protestants and Catholics will be able to join hands and sing in the words of that old Negro spiritual, "Free at last! Free at last! Thank God almighty, we are free at last!"

Martin Luther King, 1963

To be black and conscious in America is to be in a constant state of rage.

James Baldwin, writer

The price of the liberation of the white people is the liberation of the blacks—the total liberation, in the cities, in the towns, before the law and in the mind.

James Baldwin, 1963

The cornerstones of the country's operation are economic and political strength and power. The black man does not have the economic strength—and it will take time for him to build it. But right now the American black man has the political strength and power to change his destiny overnight.

Malcolm X, 1965

The spirit we seek to build among black people is not a capitalistic one. It is a society in which the spirit of community and humanistic love prevail. The love we seek to encourage is within the black community, the only American community where man call each other "brother" when they meet.

Stokely Carmichael, 1966

Our will to live must no longer supersede our will to fight, for our fighting will determine if our race shall live.

H. Rap Brown, 1967

The white man makes all the laws, he drags us before his courts, he accuses us, and he sits in judgment over us.

H. Rap Brown, 1967

We live in the jaws of the exploiting octopus. We are a colony in his eyes. Our duty is clear. Our historical role is evident.

Student Non-violent
Coordinating Committee, 1968

There are those who would like to take the revolutionary sting away from black power and make it merely another American reform movement . . . It is necessary to state that Black Power is a revolutionary force that seeks the elimination of capitalism and the industrial-military complex which undergirds it.

Student Non-violent
Coordinating Committee, 1968

The only politics relevant to black people is the politics of revolution. The politics of culture is not in itself revolution . . . People can get so hooked up in their culture and their egos so inflated about being black that they have no desire to fight.

H. Rap Brown

We think that anybody who talks about black capitalism or black control of black communities in a system of international imperialism is insane.

Phil Hutchings,
Student Non-violent Coordinating
Committee, 1968

Can whites, particularly liberal whites, condemn themselves? Can they stop blaming us (blacks) and blame their own system? Are they capable of the shame which might become a revolutionary emotion?

Stokely Carmichael, 1966

Integration speaks not at all to the problem of poverty; only to the problem of blackness.

Stokely Carmichael, 1966

The economic foundations of this country must be shaken if black people are to control their lives. The colonies of the U.S.—and this includes the black ghettoes within its borders, north and south —must be liberated. For a century this nation has been like an octopus of exploitation stretching from Mississippi to

Harlem to South America, the Middle East, southern Africa and Vietnam; . . . the essential result has been the same—a powerful few have been maintained and enriched at the expense of the poor. As its grip loosens here and there around the world the hopes of black Americans become more realistic. For racism to die, a totally different America must be born.

Stokely Carmichael, 1966

(White liberals) . . . do not see that until the black man speaks for himself, leads himself, decides for himself, and even makes mistakes for himself, there will be no true equality.

James Tillman,
Psychologist, 1968

. . . no Slave should die a natural death. There is a point where caution ends and cowardice begins. Give me a bullet through the brain from the beleagured oppressor on the night of seige. Why is there dancing and singing in the Slave Quarter? A slave who dies of natural causes cannot balance two dead flies on the Scales of Eternity. Such a one deserves rather to be pitied than mourned.

Eldridge Cleaver, 1968

The black man has come to the realization that to be free, it is necessary for him to throw his life—everything—on the line . . .

Eldridge Cleaver, 1968

We shall have our manhood. We shall have it or the earth will be leveled by our attempts to gain it.

Eldridge Cleaver, 1968

Black and white, the young rebels are free people, free in a way that Americans have never been before . . . And they are outraged. There is in American today a generation of white youth that is truly worthy of a black man's respect, and this is a rare event in the foul annals of American history.

Eldridge Cleaver, 1968

V. WAR, MILITARISM AND IMPERIALISM

Even in publick military service, or warlike Expeditions by National authority, the law manifestly requires the Soldier to think for himself; and to consider before he acts in any war, whether the same be just for, if it be otherwise, the Common Law of the Kingdom will impute to him the Guilt of Murder.

Granville Sharp, 1773

The cause of America is in a great measure the cause of all mankind. Many circumstances have and will arise which are not local but universal, and through which the principles of all lovers of mankind are affected and in the event of which their affections are interested. The laying a country desolate with fire and sword, declaring war against the natural rights of all mankind, and extirpating the defenders thereof from the face of the earth is the concern of every man to whom nature has given the power of feeling . . .

Thomas Paine, pamphleteer, 1776

Nor is it, Sir, for the defense of his own house and home, that he who is the subject of military draft is to perform the task allotted to him. You will put him upon a service equally foreign to his interests and abhorrent to his feelings. With his aid you are to push the purpose of conquest. The battles which he is to fight are the battles of invasion.

Daniel Webster, 1814

Where is it written in the Constitution, in what article or section is it contained, that you may take children from their parents, and parents from their children, and compel them to fight the battles of any war, in which the folly or wickedness of Government may engage it?

Daniel Webster, 1814

A free government with an uncontrolled power of military conscription is the most ridiculous and abominable contradiction and nonsense that ever entered into the head of man.

Daniel Webster, 1814

We are the aggressors. We must cease to be the aggressors.

Charles Sumner,
U.S. Senator, 1846

We Americans have no commission from God to police the world.

Benjamin Harrison,
President, 1888

Hands acrost th' sea and into some wan's pocket.

Finley Peter Dunne (Mr. Dooley)

The great foe of democracy now and in the near future is plutocracy. Every year that passes brings out this antagonism more distinctly. It is to be the social war of the twentieth century. In that war, militarism, expansionism, and imperialism will favor plutocracy. In the first place, war and expansion will favor jobbery both in the dependencies and at home. In the second place, they will take away the attention of people from what the plutocrats are doing. In the third place, they will cause large expenditures of the people's money, the return of

54

which will not go into the Treasury, but into the hands of the few schemers. In the fourth place, they will call for a large public debt and taxes, and these things especially tend to make men unequal because any social burdens bear more heavily on the weak than on the strong . . . Therefore expansionism and imperialism are a grand onslaught on democracy.

William Graham Sumner,
Anti-imperialist, 1899

I am an anti-imperialist. I am opposed to having the eagle put its talons on any other land.

Mark Twain, 1899

(Sung to the tune of *John Brown's Body*)
In a sordid slime harmonious, Greed was born in yonder ditch;

With a longing in his bosom, for other's goods and itch;

Christ died to make men holy; let men
die to make us rich.

Our God (Greed) is marching on.

Mark Twain, 1901

We have crushed a deceived and con-
fiding people; we have turned against the
weak and friendless who trusted us; we
have invited our clean young men to
shoulder a musket and do bandits' work
under a flag which bandits have been ac-
customed to fear, not to follow.

Mark Twain, on the invasion
of the Philippines, 1901

O Lord our Father, our young patriots,
idols of our hearts, go forth to battle—be
thou near them! With them—in spirit—
we also go forth from the sweet peace of
our beloved firesides to smite the foe. O
Lord, Our God, help us tear their sold-

iers to bloody shreds with our shells; help us to cover their smiling fields with the pale forms of their patriot dead; help us to drown the thunder of their guns with the shrieks of their wounded, writhing in pain; help us to lay waste their humble homes with a hurricane of fire; help us to wring the hearts of their unoffending widows with unavailing grief; help us to turn them out roofless with their little children to wander unfriended the wastes of the desolated land in rags and hunger and thirst . . .

Mark Twain's "War Prayer," 1905

I took the canal zone and let Congress debate, and while the debate goes on the canal does also.

Thoedore Roosevelt, 1911

(I) would no more teach school children military training than teach them arson, robbery or assassination.

Eugene Debs, 1916

57

The few who profit from the labor of the masses want to organize the workers into an army which will protect the interests of the capitalists.

Helen Keller, 1916

The poor, sir, who are the ones called upon to rot in the trenches, have no organized power, have no press to voice their will upon the question of peace or war; but, oh . . . at sometime they will be heard when those who pay taxes come to have their taxes doubled and again doubled to pay the interest on the nontaxable bonds held by Morgan and his combinations. They will have their day and they will be heard. It will be as certain and as inevitable as the return of the tides, and as resistless too.

Robert M. La Follette,
U. S. Senator, 1917

The master class has always declared the war; the subject class has always fought the battles.

Eugene Debs, 1918

War is a racket.

Smedley Butler, Commanding
General U.S. Marine Corps, 1934

I was a gangster for Wall Street: I helped make Mexico and especially Tampico safe for American oil interest in 1914; I helped make Haiti and Cuba a decent place for the National City Bank boys to collect revenue in; I helped purify Nicaragua for the international banking house of Brown Bros. in 1909-12; I brought light to the Dominican Republic for American sugar interests in 1916; and I helped make Honduras "right" for American fruit companies in 1903.

Smedley Butler, Commanding
General, U.S. Marine Corps

If we see that Germany is winning we ought to help Russia, and if we see Russia is winning, we ought to help Germany, and that way let them kill as many as possible.

Harry Truman, U.S. Senator, 1941

With about five percent of the world's people, we consume about half the world's goods. We take a richness that is in good part not our own, and we put it in our pockets, our garages, our split levels, our bellies, and our futures.

Carl Oglesby, 1965

VI. WOMEN'S LIBERATION

If particular care and attention are not paid to the ladies we are determined to foment a rebellion and will not hold ourselves bound to obey any laws in which we have no voice or representation.

Abigail Adams to
husband John, 1776

No woman can forfeit her individual rights or independent existence, and no man assert over her any rights or power whatsoever beyond what he may exercise over her free and voluntary affection.

Fanny Wright, 1827

My aim is to make myself a true woman, one worthy of the name and not to be one of the delicate little dolls or the silly fools who make up the bulk of American women, slaves to society and fashion.

Anonymous feminist,
19th Century

It is quite certain that unless we have the female sex on our side we cannot hope to accomplish any object we have in view.

Seth Luther,
Labor organizer, 1830s

As our fathers resisted unto blood the lordly avarice of the British ministry . . . so we their daughters never will wear the yoke which has been prepared for us. We would rather die in the alms houses than yield to the wicked oppression attempted to be imposed upon us.

Factory Girls Assn., 1835

The history of mankind is a history of repeated injuries and usurpations on the part of man toward woman, having in direct object the establishment of absolute tyranny over her . . . He has created a false public sentiment by giving to the world a different code of morals for men and women, by which moral deliquencies which exclude women from society, are not only tolerated, but deemed of little account in man. He has endeavored in every way that he could to destroy her confidence in her powers, to lessen her self-respect, and to make her willing to lead a dependent and abject life.

Declaration of Sentiments passed
at Women's Rights Convention,
Seneca Falls, N. Y., 1848

Many who have at last made the discovery that the Negroes have some rights as well as other members of the human family, have yet to be convinced that women are entitled to any.

Frederick Douglass, 1848

Women of Ohio! Whose cheek does not blush, whose blood does not tingle at this cool lawyer-like recital of the gross injustices and wrongs which Government has heaped upon our sex? With these marks of inferiority branded upon our persons . . . how can we rise to true dignity of human nature? No wonder that so many of our politicians are dough faced serviles, without independence of manhood; no wonder our priests are time-serving and sycophantic; no wonder that so many men are moral cowards and cringing poltroons. What more could be expected of progeny of slaves? Slaves are we, politically and legally. How can we, who it is said are educators of our children, present to this nation anything else but a generation of

serviles, while we ourselves are in a ser-
vile condition and padlocks are on our
lips?

J. Elizabeth Jones, 1849

Resolved: that the speedy success of
our cause depends on the zealous and un-
tiring efforts of both men and women for
the overthrow of the monopoly of the pulpit and for the securing to women an
equal participation with men in the various trades, professions and commerce.

Lucrecia Mott, feminist leader

Will it be answered that we are fac-
tious, discontented spirits, striving to
disturb the public order, and tear up the
old fastnesses of society? So it was said of
Jesus Christ . . . So it was said of our
forefathers . . . So it has been said of every
reform . . . We fear not man as an enemy.

He is our friend, our brother. Let woman speak for herself and she will be heard.

Frances D. Gage, feminist, 1851

Why if I were a woman and believed that she who is a wife and a mother must be nothing more but must cramp her thoughts into the narrow circle of her own home and indulge no grander aspiration for universal interests—believing that, I would forswear marriage.

Cleveland Women's Rights
Convention, Henry Blackwell,
Speaker, 1853

In education, in marriage, in everything, disappointment is the lot of woman. It shall be the business of my life to deepen this disappointment in every woman's heart until she bows down to it no longer.

Lucy Stone, 1855

Give your heaviest raps on the head of every Nabob who does injustice to a human being for the crime of color or sex!

Susan B. Anthony

Woman is made the slave of a slave and is reckoned fit only for companionship in lust. The hands and breasts that nursed all men into life are scorned as the forgetful brute proclaims his superior strength. Man's superiority will be shown, not in the fact that he has enslaved his wife, but in that he has made her free.

Eugene Debs

VII. STUDENTS AND SCHOOLS

Every age and generation must be as free to act for itself, *in all cases*, as the ages and generation which preceded it . . . Man has no property in man; neither has any generation a property in the generations which are to follow.

Thomas Paine, 1776

As a nation we have too long educated the mind, and left the *heart* a moral waste.

Angelina Grimke, 1837

In most if not all of our American colleges the truth is denied a hearing and excluded from the classroom if it seems to conflict with the selfish interests of the moneyed classes—from whom endowments are to be expected.

Willis J. Abbot, journalist, 1899

The good Lord gave me my money, and how could I withhold it from the University of Chicago?

John D. Rockefeller

As I look over the universities of my land . . . I see the students asleep . . . asleep in the face of the awful facts . . . asleep in the greatest revolution that has ever come . . . University men and women, you men and women in the full glory of life, here is a cause that appeals to all the romance in you. Awake to its call. Line up! Line up! All the world despises a coward. Read our books. Fight us if you

do not agree . . . But by all that is brave
and strong show your colors.

Jack London, author, 1905

I found the University . . . clean and
noble, but I did not find the university
alive. I found the American university
had this ideal as phrased by a professor
in Chicago University: "The passionless
pursuit of passionless intelligence"—
clean and noble, I grant you, but not alive
enough . . . And in the reflection of this
University ideal I find the conservatism
and unconcern of the American people
toward those who are suffering, who are
in want."

Jack London, 1906

Youth rules the world, but only when it
is no longer young. It is a tarnished, tra-
vestied youth that is in the saddle in the
person of middle age. Old age lives in the

delusion that it has improved and rationalized its youthful ideas by experience and stored up wisdom, when all it has done is to damage them—more or less—usually more. And the tragedy of life is that the world is run by those damaged ideals.

Randolph Bourne, essayist, 1913

College isn't the place to go for ideas.

Helen Keller, 1916

The "futures" and careers" for which American students now prepare are . . . intellectual and moral wastelands. This chrome-plated consumers paradise would have us grow up to be well-behaved children. But an important minority of men and women coming to the front today have shown that they will die rather than be standardized, replaceable and irrelevant.

Mario Savio, 1964

Our professors and administrators sacrifice controversy to public relations; their curriculums change more slowly than the living events of the world; their skills and silence are purchased by investors in the arms race; passion is called unscholastic.

The Port Huron Statement
Founding of Students for a
Democratic Society, 1965

Do not wish to be a student in contrast to being a man. Do not study as a student, but as a man who is alive and who cares. Leave the isolated world of ideological fantasy, allow your ideas to become part of your living and your living to become part of your ideas.

Tom Hayden, 1962

VIII. THE PRESS

The press does not speak the voice of the nation. It does not even speak the voice of those who write for it.

Fanny Wright, 1829

As for the newspapers, I do not chance to know one in the country that will deliberately print anything that will ultimately and permanently reduce the numbers of its subscribers. They do not believe it would be expedient. If we do not say pleasant things, they argue, nobody will attend to us.

Henry David Thoreau, 1859

The modern newspaper is half ads and the other half lies between the ads.

Anonymous

The very moment the capitalist press credits me with being a wise labor leader, I will invite you to investigate me upon the charge of treason.

Eugene Debs, 1905

The money power behind the newspapers is against socialism, and the editors, obedient to the hand that feeds them, will go to any length to put down socialism.

Helen Keller, 1911

We're not interested in a good press. We're interested in becoming free.

Robert Williams,
Black nationalist, 1962

IX. ON VOTING

Even voting for *the right* is *doing nothing* for it. It is only expressing to men feebly your desire that it should prevail.

Henry David Thoreau, 1849

No reform is possible within the existing parties. History has proven that no reform was ever yet worked inside the party or sect in which originated the corruption complained of.

Stephen Smith, Secy.
Farmer State Assn. of Ill., 1873

The ballot box is simply a capitalist concession.

Thomas J. Hagerty,
Labor organizer, 1905

Voting for socialism is not socialism any more than a menu is a meal.

Eugene Debs, 1911

We the people are not free. Our democracy is but a name. We vote? What does that mean? It means that we choose between Tweedledum and Tweedledee. We elect expensive masters to do our work for us, and then blame them because they work for themselves and for their class.

Helen Keller, 1911

Vote in the streets!

Students for a Democratic
Society, 1968

X. PATRIOTISM

Guard against the postures of pretended patriotism.

George Washington, 1796

There is still another influence which stimulates war, and interferes with the natural atractions of Peace; I refer to a selfish and exaggerated *love of country*, leading to its physical aggrandizement and political exaltation at the expense of other countries, and in disregard of the principles of True Greatness . . . Men are taught to live, not for mankind, but only for a small portion of mankind. The pride, vanity, ambition, brutality even, which we rebuke in individuals are accounted virtues when displayed in the name of country.

Charles Sumner,
U.S. Senator, 1845

Worse than traitors in arms are the men who pretending loyalty to the Flag, feast and fatten on the misfortunes of the nation.

Congressional committee
report, 1863

My kind of loyalty was loyalty to one's country, not to its institutions or its office-holders. The country is the real thing . . . to watch over. . . Institutions are extraneous, they are its mere clothing and clothing can wear out or become ragged . . . To be loyal to rags, that is the loyalty of unreason. It is pure animal. The citizen who thinks he sees that the commonwealth's political clothes are worn out, and yet, holds his peace, and does not agitate for a new suit, is disloyal; he is a traitor. That he may be the only one who thinks he sees this decay, does not excuse him; it is his duty to agitate anyway.

Mark Twain

Loyalty to petrified opinions never yet broke a chain or freed a human soul in *this* world—and never will.

Mark Twain, 1885

If Fascism came to America it would be on a program of Americanism.

Huey P. Long, governor and
senator from Louisiana, 1935

Many a bum show has been saved by the flag.

George M. Cohan, showman

XI. LIBERALS AND LIBERALISM

Words may show a man's wit, but ac-
tions his meaning.

Benjamin Franklin

We talk of friendship with those in
whom our reason forbids us to have faith,
and our affection, wounded through a
thousand pores, instructs us to detest is
madness and folly . . . Ye that tell us of
harmony and reconciliation, can ye restore to us the time that is past? Can ye
give to prostitution its former innocence?

Thomas Paine, 1776

Toleration is not the opposite of intoleration, but is the counterfeit of it. Both are despotisms. The one assumes to itself the right of withholding liberty of conscience, and the other of granting it. The one is the Pope armed with fire and faggot, and the other is the Pope selling or granting indulgences.

Thomas Paine, 1791

'Tis the business of little minds to shrink, but he whose heart is firm and whose conscience approves his conduct will pursue his principles unto death.

Thomas Paine, 1776

There are persons . . . who see not the full extent of the evil which threatens them; they solace themselves with hopes that the enemy, if he succeed, will be merciful. It is the madness of folly to expect mercy from those who have refused to do justice; and even mercy, where conquest is the object is only a trick of war; the cunning of the fox is as murderous as the violence of the wolf, and we ought to guard equally against both.

Thomas Paine, 1776

As for conforming outwardly, and living your own life inwardly, I do not think much of that.

Henry David Thoreau, 1850

Some (of my neighbors) seemed really glad to see the work go on, if somebody else would do it.

Levi Coffin, "president"
Underground Railroad

It is easier to sit on the heights of criticism, and look down with a scrutinizing eye upon the work done by others, which we ought to have done ourselves, and to say, "but for these rude guns, I would be a soldier."

Wendell Phillips, 1850

Caution, caution, sir! It is nothing but the word of cowardice.

John Brown, abolitionist

Cautious, careful people always casting about to preserve their reputation and social standards, never can bring about a reform. Those who are really in earnest must be willing to be anything or nothing in the world's estimation and publicly and privately, in season and out, avow their sympathies with despised ideas and their advocates, and bear the consequences.

Susan B. Anthony

A liberal is a man who leaves a room when the fight begins.

Heywood Broun, journalist

I don't give a damn about semi-radicals.

Helen Keller, 1916

The peaceful and indifferent are forgotten; they never know the fighting joy of living.

Elizabeth Gurley Flynn, 1917

True, we didn't tie the knot in Mississippi and we didn't pull the trigger in Viet Nam—that is, we personally—but we've been standing behind the knot tiers and the trigger pullers too long.

Ellen, one of the Mississippi
Summer Project volunteers, 1964

XII. LAW AND ORDER

Whatever the apparent cause of any riots may be, the real one is always want of happiness. It shows that something is wrong in the system of government that injures the felicity by which society is to be preserved.

Thomas Paine, 1792

The poor have no laws. The laws are made by the rich and of course for the rich.

Working People of New Castle
County, Delaware, 1829

We should be men first and subjects afterward. It is not desirable to cultivate a respect for the law, so much as for the right.

Henry David Thoreau

The highest virtue is always against the law.

Ralph Waldo Emerson, essayist

We preserve the so-called peace of our community by deeds of violence every day. Look at the policeman's billy and handcuffs. Look at the jail. Look at the gallows. Look at the chaplain of the regiment.

Henry David Thoreau, 1859

Courts of arbitration are nonsense. I don't want any. Of what use are they when the commissioners are paid and bribed by the capitalists to decide against us? Away with them! Do business with the devil and you'll be swindled. We want the full value of our labor—that's all.

Walter Vrooman, *Workmen's Advocate*, 1887

As a revolutionist I have no respect for capitalist property laws, nor the least scruple about violating them. I hold all such laws to have been enacted through chicanery, fraud and corruption. But this does not imply that I propose making an individual law-breaker of myself and battling my head against the stone wall of existing property laws. That might be called force, but it would be more than that. It would be mere weakness and folly.

Eugene Debs, 1912

I did violate every one of your laws and still come before you and say: to hell with the courts—because I believe my right to live is far more sacred than the sacred right of property that you and your kind so ably defend.

Worker to Judge, 1915

A demonstration of working men in the interests of the constitutional right of freedom of speech is judged a riot by the courts; but violence and terrorism on the part of the capitalists and their tools is "law and order."

Industrial Worker, 1918

The wise fools who sit in the high places of justice fail to see that in revolutionary times vital issues are settled not by statutes, decrees and authorities, but in spite of them.

Helen Keller, 1919

Capitalism is proud of its prisons which fitly sumbolize the character of its institutions and constitute one of the chief elements in its philanthropy.

Eugene Debs, 1927

What interests me is how a guy could have on a policeman's uniform and still be like me, yet have the power to hit me on the head when he felt like it.

Arthur Dunmeyer,
Harlem street hustler, 1966

The policeman isn't there to create disorder. He's there to preserve disorder.

Richard J. Daley,
Mayor of Chicago, 1968

"Justice" in this country means "just-us white folks."

H. Rap Brown

When government becomes the law-breaker then people must become the law enforcers.

H. Rap Brown

There are times when order must be maintained because order must be maintained.

Grayson Kirk, former president
of Columbia University, 1968

The police are the armed guardians of the social order. The blacks are the chief domestic victims of the American social order. A conflict of interest exists, therefore, between the blacks and the police. It is not solely a matter of trigger-happy cops, of brutal cops who love to crack black heads. Mostly it's a job to them. It pays good. And there are numerous fringe benefits. The real problem is a trigger-happy social order.

Eldridge Cleaver, 1968

XIII. SELF DEFENSE AND VIOLENCE

It is the violence which is done and threatened to our persons, the destruction of our property by armed force, the invasion of our country by fire and sword which conscientiously qualifies the use of arms.

Thomas Paine, 1776

. . . had you not rather be killed than to be a slave to a tyrant who takes the life of your mother, wife and dear little children? . . . It is no more harm for you to kill a man, who is trying to kill you, than it is for you to take a drink of water when thirsty.

David Walker,
Abolitionist, 1828

I am sure that the American slaves have the natural moral right to rise in insurrection and cut their masters' throats for the sake of their freedom . . . and the time may come when it will be their natural, moral duty to do so; if I were held bondage as they are, in the center of the continent and a file of men two thousand miles long stood between me and my natural liberty, then I would split that threat of life from end to end and secure my natural right to liberty even if I hewed down a man at every step, and walked blood red from Texas to Canada! Why, what means that pile of stone at Bunker Hill? What the celebration of the great days of the revolution and the memory of its men?

Rev. Theodore Parker,
Abolitionist, 1832

Insurrection of thought always precedes insurrection of arms.

Wendell Phillips, 1859

The only penetrable point of a tyrant is fear of death.

Frederick Douglass, 1860

Dynamite! Of all the good stuff that is the stuff! . . . Place this in the immediate vicinity of a lot of rich loafers who live by the sweat of other people's brows, and light the fuse. A most cheerful and gratifying result will follow . . . A pound of this good stuff beats a bushel of ballots all hollow—and don't you forget it. Our lawmakers might as well try to sit down on the crater of a volcano or on a point of a bayonet as to endeavor to stop the manufacture and use of dynamite.

Albert Parsons, 1885

I don't know of anything that can be applied that will bring as much satisfaction to you, as much anguish to the boss as a little sabotage in the right place at the proper time.

Bill Haywood, 1909

To try to settle the question of "just what we will do on the day after the general strike" is like a man with black hair trying to foretell just when his hair will turn gray. Time alone will tell.

Industrial Worker,
I. W. W. Newspaper, 1910

I don't mean to say that we advocate violence; but we won't tell our members to allow themselves to be shot down and beaten up like cattle. Violence as a general rule is forced on us.

Vincent St. John, I.W.W., 1911

More than one organization has died settling tactics.

Industrial Worker, 1912

The protection the government owes you and fails to provide, you are morally bound to provide for yourselves . . . when the law fails and becomes the bulwark of crime and oppression, then an appeal to force is not only morally justified, but becomes a patriotic duty.

Eugene Debs, 1914

The principle of self defense is an American tradition that began at Lexington and Concord.

Robert Williams,
Black nationalist, 1962

It is criminal to teach a man not to defend himself when he is the constant victim of brutal attacks.

Malcolm X

Social change is violence itself. You cannot have progress without friction and upheaval. For social change, two systems must clash. This must be a violent clash, because it's a struggle for survival for one and a struggle for liberation of the other. And always the powers in command are ruthless and unmerciful in defending their position and their privileges.

Robert Williams, 1962

The United States spends more on instruments of violence and a class of specialists in violence than any other country. The stern-faced generals on pedestals in our park; the aimless brutality of the animated cartoons; the endless flow of grenades, rockets and burp guns to amuse the children; and the bloody fairy tales of television are random illustrations of the same point.

Richard J. Barnet,
Anti-imperialist, 1968

You don't have a revolution in which you love your enemy. And you don't have a revolution in which you are begging the system of exploitation to integrate you into it.

Malcolm X, 1964

Revolutions do not take place in velvet boxes. They never have. It is only the poets who make them lovely.

Carl Oglesby, 1965

XIV. DARE TO STRUGGLE

We Dare Be Free

> Motto of the Sons of Liberty,
> 1774

If I am to have a master, let me have a severe one that I may always have the mortifying sense of it. I shall then always be disposed to take the first fair opportunity of ridding myself of slavery.

> Samuel Adams,
> Revolutionary leader, 1772

Gentlemen may cry peace, peace—but there is no peace . . . What would they have? Is life so dear, or peace so sweet, as to be purchased at the prices of chains and slavery?

Patrick Henry, 1775

If our people fight one tribe at a time, all will be killed. They can cut off our fingers one by one, but if we join together we will make a powerful fist.

Little Turtle, Master General
of the Miami Indians, 1791

Only people with empty heads feast while their hearts should be heavy with grief.

Mangus Colorado, Apache chief

. . . nature's God commands the slave to rise, and on th' oppressor's head to break his chain.

John Quincy Adams

Tell a man whose house is on fire to give a moderate alarm; tell him to moderately rescue his wife from the hands of the ravisher; tell the mother to gradually extricate her babe from the fire into which it has fallen . . .

> William Lloyd Garrison,
> Abolitionist, 1831

One man with courage makes a majority.

> Andrew Jackson,
> U.S. President

I will be as harsh as Truth and as uncompromising as Justice.

> William Lloyd Garrison, 1831

If there is no struggle, there is no progress. Those who profess to freedom and yet deprecate agitation are men who want crops without plowing. They want rain without thunder and lightning. They want the ocean without the awful roar of its mighty waters. This struggle may be a moral one, or it may be physical, but it must be a struggle. Power concedes nothing without a demand. It never did and it never will.

Frederick Douglass, 1857

There are a thousand hacking at the branches of evil to one who is striking at the root.

Henry David Thoreau, 1858

Slavery shall go down even if it must be put down with red swords.

John Brown, abolitionist, 1858

I pity the poor in bondage that have none to help them, that is why I am here;

not to gratify any personal animosity, revenge, or vindictive spirit. It is my sympathy with the oppressed and the wronged, that are as good as you, and as precious in the sight of God.

John Brown, 1859

I think you can make a better use of iron than forging it into chains. If you must have the metal, put it into Sharpe's rifles. It is a great deal better used that way than in fetters.

Wendell Phillips, abolitionist, 1859

If it is deemed necessary that I should forfeit my life for the furtherance of the ends of justice, and mingle blood further with the blood of my children and with the blood of millions in this slave country whose rights are disregarded by wicked, cruel and unjust enactments, I say, let it be done . . .

John Brown, 1859

"Do what the spirit say do."

Negro spiritual

Men are whipped oftenest who are whipped easiest.

Frederick Douglass, 1866

Under a government which imprisons any unjustly, the true place for a just man is also in prison . . . If any think that their influence would be lost there, and their voices no longer afflict the ear of the State, that they would not be as an enemy within its walls, they do not know by how much and effectively he can combat injustice who has experienced a little in prison . . . A minority is powerless while it conforms to the majority; it is not even a minority then; but it is irresistable when it clogs by its whole weight. If the alternative is to keep all just men in prison or give up war and slavery, the State will not hesitate to choose.

Henry David Thoreau, 1879

What you farmers need to do is raise less corn and more hell!

Mary Elizabeth Lease,
Kansas populist, 1890

We are an island of Indians in a lake of whites. We must stand together, or they will rub us out separately. These soldiers have come up shooting; they want war. All right; we'll give it to them.

Sitting Bull, 1878

Let it be recorded that I was the last man of my people to lay down my gun.*

Sitting Bull, 1881

The voice of protest, of warning, of appeal is never more in need than when the clamor of fife and drum, echoed by the press and too often by the pulpit, is bidding all men fall in and keep step and obey in silence the tyrannous word of command.

Charles Eliot Norton,
Educator, 1898

* It is stated today that there was a quiet understanding between the officers of the Indian and Military Departments that it would be impossible to bring Sitting Bull to Standing Rock alive, and that if brought in, nobody would know precisely what to do with him. There was, therefore, cruel as it may seem, a complete understanding from the Commanding Officer to the Indian Police that the slightest attempt to rescue the old medicine man should be a signal to send Sitting Bull to the happy hunting ground.

New York Herald, Dec. 17, 1880

Don't let the bastards grind you down.

Joseph Stilwell, U.S. General

Let the voice of the people be heard.

Albert Parsons, labor agitator,
last words at execution, 1887

Open your mouths and let out your lungs, raise such a clamor that those in high places will wonder what all the row is about and perchance feel tottering under them the edifices of greed they have reared.

Jack London, writer, 1905

We learn to fight by fighting.

Mary Marcy, Industrial Workers
of the World, 1911

Goodbye, Bill: I die like a true rebel. Don't waste any time mourning—organize! It is a hundred miles from here to Wyoming. Could you arrange to have my body hauled to the state line to be buried? I don't want to be found dead in Utah.

Joe Hill, 1915, last letter to
Bill Heywood.

I would rather a thousand times be a free soul in jail than to be a sycophant and coward in the streets. If it had not been for the men and women who, in the past, have had the moral courage to go to jail, we would still be in the jungles.

Eugene Debs, 1918

. . . while there is a lower class I am in it, while there is a criminal element I am of it, and while there is a soul in prison I am not free.

Eugene Debs, 1918

When great changes occur in history, when great principles are involved as a rule the majority are wrong. The minority are usually right. In every age there have been a few heroic souls who have been misunderstood, maligned, persecuted, sometimes put to death. Washington, Jefferson, Franklin, Paine . . . were the rebels of their day. When they began to chafe under the rule of a foreign king and to sow the seed of resistance among the colonists they were opposed by the people and denounced by the press.

Eugene Debs, 1918

History shows that no master class is ever willing to let go without a quarrel. The capitalists own the government's armies, and the militia. Don't you think the capitalists will use these institutions to keep themselves in power? I do.

Jack London, 1923

. . . if you keep on taking aspirin long enough it will cease to deaden pain. And that is when the fun begins. That is when you begin to notice that snow isn't beautiful at all. That is when your hair begins to freeze and you begin to get up in the middle of the night, laughing quietly, waiting for the worst, remembering all the pain, not wanting any longer to be half-dead, wanting full death or full life. That is when you begin to be mad about the way things are going in this country . . . . That is when, weak as you are, something old and savage, and defiant in you comes up bitterly out of your illness and starts to smash things, pushing you into the sun, getting you away from evasions, dragging you by your neck to life.

William Saroyan, 1934

Power never takes a back step—only in the face of more power. Power doesn't back up in the face of a smile or in the face of a threat, or in the face of some kind of nonviolent loving action. It's not the nature of power to back up in the face of anything but some more power. Power recognizes only power, and all of them who realize this have made gains.

Malcolm X

Never do anything against conscience even if the State demands it.

Albert Einstein, physicist

We've talked about it long enough. Let's do something.

Joseph McNeill, 17,
just before first Southern
sit-in, Wilmington, N. C., 1960

Let the old women complain wisely about the "end of ideology." We are beginning to move again.

C. Wright Mills, 1960

The future belongs to today's oppressed.

Robert Williams,
Black nationalist, 1962

There is a time when the operation of
the machine becomes so odious, makes
you so sick at heart that you can't take
part; you can't even tacitly take part,
and you've got to put your bodies upon
the levers, upon all the apparatus, and
you've got to make it stop. And you've
got to indicate to the people who run it,
to the people who own it, that unless
you're free the machine will be prevent-
ed from working at all.

Mario Savio, 1964

I have chosen to be outside of society
after having been very much inside. I
intend to fight that society which lied
to and smothered me for so long, and con-

tinues to do so to vast numbers of people
. . . I believe in freedom and must take
the jump; I must take the chance of
action.

Anon, White SNCC workers, 1964

Being a man is the continuing battle of
one's life. One loses a bit of manhood with
every stale compromise to the authority
of any power in which one does not believe. No slave should die a natural
death. There is a point where caution
ends and cowardice begins. Every day I
am in prison I will refuse both food and
water . . . My hunger is for the liberation
of my people; my thirst is for the ending of
oppression.

H. Rap Brown, 1968

The spirit of the people is greater than
the Man's technology.

Huey P. Newton, 1968

Our analysis of the country tells us that we must begin, somehow, to reach more poor and working whites if we are to build a powerful radical movement. So, we urge other radicals to take a step into America —it isn't so bad. Confront White America; give poor and working people an alternative to Wallace, Reagan and Kennedy; build for the revolution—it's out there!

Michael James,
Community organizer, 1967